Chicken Fat

poems by

Barbara Krasner

Finishing Line Press
Georgetown, Kentucky

Chicken Fat

ACKNOWLEDGMENTS

Blue Lyra Review, "Bei Mir Bistu Shayn"
Naugatuck River Review, "When I Dream of Twisters"
The Jewish Writing Project, "The Circle of Life," "Bearing Witness"
Jewish Woman's Literary Annual, "The Granit"
Minerva Rising, "My Mother Was Dead"
Montclair Historical Society, "Quilted"
Paterson Literary Review, "Grandma Ruth," "Because I'm Jewish"
Rose Red Review, "Elegy to Aunt Jo"
Tiferet, "Chicken Fat"

Publisher: Leah Maines

Editor: Christen Kincaid

Cover Art: Barbara Krasner

Author Photo: Picture People

Cover Design: Elizabeth Maines McCleavy

Printed in the USA on acid-free paper.
Order online: www.finishinglinepress.com
            also available on amazon.com

Author inquiries and mail orders:
Finishing Line Press
P. O. Box 1626
Georgetown, Kentucky 40324
U. S. A.

Table of Contents

Chicken Fat

Chicken fat smells like mincing onions
in a cherrywood bowl with metal chopper.
Chicken fat smells like roast chicken smeared
on a slab of pumpernickel, the way Grandma
used to give my mother lunch in a paper bag
for walks to Bath Beach with Bubba Esther.

Chicken fat smells like Brooklyn and dark hallways
with hand-me-down bicycles, a brick stoop
and concrete walk. Chicken fat smells of closed doors
and embroidered table cloths over plain tables
for Rosh Hashonah, like starched white clothes
and scrub-brushed hands for Shabbos. It smells
of Grandma Ruth's fuzzy slippers on the kitchen
linoleum, her feet too swollen for proper shoes.
Chicken fat smells of mah-jongg and face powder
on ladies smoking and yakking while their husbands
work. Chicken fat smells of Thursday deliveries
from Seroff's of Irvington and unbundling poultry
and meat from their waxed brown paper envelopes.

Chicken fat smells, bouquet of onions carmelizing
in blue marble frying pan, of a tradition from the other side
of the pond, a habit not broken by immigration
or Holocaust. Chicken fat smells like *Frume* Sarah
from the grave, like Vicks Vapo-Rub on the chest,
like an ankle sock filled with salt and held to the ear
to ease the pain. It smells like fat kisses from uncles
and the tattooed numbers of Hebrew School
teachers pinching children's cheeks, saying *mamashaynele*.

Chicken fat smells like repairing the world.

Grandma Ruth

You shuffle about the kitchen you inherited
from my real grandma in your fuzzy slippers
with worn heels. You wear your love
in your pots and pans and make me
a chocolate milkshake since my parents
have abandoned me for the day and
the 1964 World's Fair. Once again I
have injured my legs and cannot go.

Back into the dark living room, you
turn on the Amana and adjust the rabbit
ears, tuning into *Lawrence Welk* on Channel 7.
It's Sunday night, but you correctly sense
I'd rather watch *The Wonderful World
of Disney* on Channel 4 and change the program.

You bring your knitting needles out of your bag
and resume making a dress for my Barbie. But
your stepson, my birth uncle, owns a toy store
and I can get all the Barbie clothes I want and
ripping open those pink and purple cardboard
holders is not the same as seeing those dull
knitted smocks with fur collars you make.

I am afraid to admit that those knitted outfits
shame me, as if we couldn't afford Barbie clothes.
I focus on the program and my milkshake because
I don't want to blurt out the truth. I don't want to make
you feel bad, because you must feel bad enough
to live in a dead woman's house and sleep
with a dead woman's husband.

I wish I had kept all those clothes you made and no one
can find your mah-jongg case. I wish I could have
given you more joy and appreciated what you gave
to a granddaughter you loved as your own.

Because I'm Jewish

I know there's a God when I'm in a plane
above the clouds and the sky is so large
I think it's God's canvas and He's held
a palette of colors you can't get at Michael's.
I know there's a God when an SUV rear-ends
me on the Garden State Parkway. Three air bags
deploy and the SUV pushes me into the Honda
in front and then into the median. There is no trunk
and no glass and when I come to, I brush myself off,
grab my purse and stagger out. Even my doctor
believes someone up there is helping me. I know
there's a God when I survive scarlet fever, meningitis,
and cancer—*keinehora, puh, puh, puh.* Not to mention
the abusive husband, and a loss of confidence
that takes me ten years to regain.

I know there's a God when my
son gets into trouble and my high school German teacher,
now guidance counselor, comes back into my life.
And when I come home after my kid is taken to jail
for burglary, Erich asks if I am all right instead
of saying like most of my family that it's all my fault.
God's hands opens Erich's as he holds me close at the Eros Café
and says I made the right decision
to send my son outward bound into the Appalachians
with an orange jumpsuit and sixty-pound backpack
to face himself and find his own Higher Power.
There must be a God, because Erich and I are still close
after forty-five years, that we believe in the same God
even though we adhere to different religions.

But where is God when my mother can't decide
to stay or go after a gall bladder surgery renders her
incoherent, speaking in Yiddish—her *mameloshn*—
and reaching out her arm to her mama? Where is God
when my ex throws our baby into the kitchen cabinets?
Where is God when my sister's husband drops dead at Applebee's?

Is it a yin and yang thing? Or do some people just
have more power, more luck, more influence with God?
Do they pray more? Do they serve more? Or is it,
as my mother used to say about anything, because I'm Jewish?

The Circle of Life

Yiddish births my mama's mother tongue
Yiddish silences my mama at death
Yiddish curls around the circle of life
Yiddish comes up from beneath the dirt
Yiddish spits, curses, and insults
Yiddish grabs like my *bubbe's* cheek pinch
It is the language I cannot speak.

Where Do I Live?

I look at the man in his blue uniform,
his shiny badge reminds me
of silver, ancient Torah shields
that keep the rabbi's place
in the scripture.
Where do you live?
What?
Where do you live?
I don't know, I say.
My bare toes grab the sand.
I am at the beach? What beach?
Five knotted dough balls, those big ones,
I wear like bracelets.
You can't sell those pretzels without
a license, the man says. Where
do you live?
I still don't know.
He could talk all he wants,
I don't understand a word.
By the looks of him, he wouldn't
understand Yiddish neither. Nothing
has been right since the Alter Kocker
died. So now you know. I can say
it. I was three years older
than him when we married.
The journey here from Poland—
or was it Russia?—
he did without me.
I came later with women
whose names I can't remember.
I can't remember.
My daughter?
My mother?
My grandchildren?
It's a haze like the horizon.

The wind snaps my naked ankles
like I'm some drying bedsheet
strung up for all to see. I'm back
in Ostrova, my *tate's* butcher shop,
the smell, the stains of animal blood,
the squawks, the bleats. Filthy white
birds peck now at my bracelets. *I want
to go home*, I tell the man.
I don't know where that is.
I long for fields,
I long for Shabbos songs.
Mama, take me home.

Generations at the Cemetery

On the only day open to the public
my father, my son, and I drive
to Newark's Grove Street Cemetery.
Police line the street, standing by
at their motorcycles. Barbed wire
fences surround the thirty-seven
sections. My father, now seventy-three,
remembers making out checks
to Ain Yankiff for his grandparents'
perpetual care. He is named
Mottel, for his grandfather. I am named
Bryna, for his grandmother. The cemetery
office tells us where the Ain Yankiff section
is, and we drive around the corner
to 19th Street, parking by Rabbi
Cohen's mausoleum. I take the hand
of my three-year-old, Matthew, his curls
damp against his neck. He toddles along
in his rainbow-suspendered jeans
and light-up sneakers. My father takes my hand,
and we count ten rows up. There
it is—Krasner—a double headstone,
baking under the relentless sun,
shadeless granite absorbing the inscriptions.

The Hebrew tells us who their fathers
were. The English tells us who once loved
them, no longer alive to mourn. Only my father
knew about Ain Yankiff. And now I know
too. I can hear Bryna sputter, "Look,
Mottel, finally someone has thought to come."
Mottel remains silent while she continues,
"And three generations, hoo-ha. Our grandson,
our great-granddaughter, and our
great-great grandson. We have been found."
But that's not the whole story, Bubbe Bryna.
By finding you I have found myself
with my father and Matthew
as witnesses. We place rocks on your graves.

A Stone for a Stone

Grandma Eva, I am sorry I lost
your mother's ring. Though the stone
was poor and puny, and I'd worn out
the inscription of her Yiddish name,
you'd left it to your eldest, and I,
his youngest, misplaced it.

I found it one day in a Dutch Masters cigar box.
Daddy had kept it in his store safe until he
retired and sold the business.

How did you come by the ring?
Did your mama give it to you when
        you left Kozlov for America?
Did your sisters mail it to you after
        your mama died and they didn't
        yet know about Auschwitz?
Did your brother safeguard it at the DP
        camp in Germany and bring it to you
        just before you died of diabetes and cancer?

Bubbe Eva, I am sorry I lost
your mother's ring. Was it all you had of her?
Was it the only reminder of thatched roofs
and your papa's butcher counter, his scale
to weigh the meat, the abacus to count
customers' change?

Did your father buy the ring from a traveling
salesman, making his way from *shtetl* to *shtetl*?
Did your papa haggle the price and get a good deal?
Did your parents host an engagement party
with peppered chick peas? Were they introduced
by the matchmaker or had they always known
each other and run to the fields
for forbidden kisses and confidences?

I shouldn't have taken the ring from the house.
I shouldn't have worn it as often as I did.
But I wanted a connection to you and your own ring
went to my sister who was named for you.

Grandma, I am sorry I lost
your mother's ring. That I betrayed your trust
even though we never met. Your eyes closed
before I became a granddaughter. I place
an extra stone, large and smooth, on your grave.

Bearing Witness

I never knew my grandmother.
I never knew why she left her Polish *shtetl*.
I never knew why she was Austro-Hungarian and Polish at the same time.
I never tasted her stuffed cabbage with raisins in white sauce.
I never ladled the *cholent* she left on the stove all day for her boys.
I never ate her boiled hot dogs on a bun on Market Day.
I never went by two buses with her to the Prince Street market.
I never sat on her knee while she kibitzed with neighbors by the front window radiator.
I never appreciated her generosity as she doled out clothing after the celluloid explosion of '33.
I never rang her cash register.
I never witnessed her haggling with Second Avenue wholesalers.
I never saw her hold fabrics between her fingers to decide what to sell in the store.
I never scolded her for wearing such thin flowered dresses.
I never noticed the flash in her eyes before a belly laugh.
I never beheld her penetrating gaze or fell victim to her caustic words.
I never addressed envelopes in English to her sisters in Europe.
I never spotted worry lines on her face with three sons in the U.S. Armed Forces.
I never accompanied her to the Joint to sponsor her only surviving relative to America.
I never visited her, wracked with cancer in the hospital.
I never felt her joy when Chaim arrived from the DP camp.
She never knew me.

Shiva

It's mid-October and the leaves have turned.
My father, shrouded in his wooden box, is buried
on Sukkot, embalmed because the holidays
got in the way.

A father, a husband, a brother, a son,
a grocer, an enthusiast for armchair travel,
advertising, publishing—he had to be more
than the man who made countless lists
and announcer of "I'll take care of that."

As we sat *shiva* in our family home, his only sister
says, "I remember when he wanted to enlist
and he needed to get his weight down." He wanted
to be an Air Force cadet.

My mother interjects, "He could never find his way
out of Washington, D.C." His classmates went out
on a mission and never returned.

My aunt picks up again, laying out the bagels,
cream cheese, smoked fishes—sable, carp, whitefish, lox.
"He was so determined. He walked and walked every day
until he qualified."

I could picture him setting out every day
despite his mama's protestations. It was winter.
There was snow. It was cold. There was work to do.

My middle sister does not join us. She lies in his bed
and won't come out. She's getting married in two weeks
and Daddy isn't here to give her away. "Maybe I should
cancel the wedding," she says, but we tell her no.

When I saw my father in his coffin, the one I picked out,
he wasn't in there. His spirit had already exited. Only
the physical shell remained, free of the pain of dialysis,
free of the intrusion of shunts. I thought of his mother
with him now, the comfort she'd give him, pinching his cheeks
and cooing *mamashaynele*. He would argue he's too old
for that now and yet he'd inch closer to her just to feel her touch.

We are sitting *shiva* and I take a serving of creamed lox,
remembering how much he liked it, our Saturday night
trips to Watson's bagel factory in Irvington and Tabatchnik's
nearby for scallion cheese and sturgeon, if we were lucky.

How little of these purchases actually made it home.

Years ago, too, my father laminated the obituary
of a younger brother. He never talked of loss.
He barely talked. He'd hang up the phone before
saying goodbye. But he was the first to arrive
when I had meningitis, barking orders at the hospital
staff to get me a blanket and a room. He came
every day of my fifteen days, sometimes after a stop
at the local diner to get my favorite, broiled veal chops.

It's *shiva* and he will never again take my hand
to cross the street, make a bad joke (What label is Bread on?
Wonder, I think), step on my mother's feet while taking
Arthur Murray dance lessons in the Catskills.

"He wrote Victory letters," my aunt says. "He never said
much. I still have them." I go down to the basement
and rummage through his desk. I find his wartime
aerial photos, his V-Day *Stars and Stripes*, the photos
of him with his mother's cousins (their families already
deported east and gassed), his letters of recommendation
for the service, and his honorable discharge papers.

I didn't know him, didn't know him at all.
All I have
is the black ribbon
pinned to my heart.

The Granit

The Adirondack chairs and weeping willows
are the first signs that we've arrived. After two
hours in our turquoise Chrysler station wagon,
along the Quickway, up the cliff that makes us
hold our breath, through Ellenville we drive to
the Granit, in Kerhonkson.

The lobby sprawls before the seven of us—my parents,
my two older sisters, my twin sister, Clara—it is filled
with ladies playing mah-jongg and cigar-smoking men
in swim trunks and short-sleeved terrycloth jackets,
sucking in their bellies as they pass that divorcee
from New Rochelle.

Connecting rooms 101 and 102 are always ours. We claimed
them with key marks along the walls, a version
of Kilroy Was Here.

Skating first and waving to Lee as we hit the ice in our stirruped
stretch pants and white sweaters with Beatle-photo'd guitar pins
over our hearts. Some Gene Pitney tune
plays through loudspeakers over the rink as my eldest
sister in her hairsprayed flip flirts with the boys.

After an hour, race you back to the room, change
into my lollipop swimsuit—"Daddy, can you please
blow up my swan?" And he holds us by the hand to the outdoor
pool. I paddle my pretend-flippers inside the swan tube
and pretend I'm beautiful. Instead, old ladies in brocaded
bathing suits hold onto the sides, they pinch my cheek and say,
"*Mamashaynele*," and I wonder what those blue markings on the
inside of their forearms mean. Their accents
remind me of Grandma and Grandpa in Brooklyn—
they always pinch my cheeks.

We dress for dinner and Clara throws my crinoline over my head
and my mother says it's a party dress, but I know it's only a slip
and I take it off. We go around and around and my mother says,
"Go without dinner," and I will, although I know Daddy will
sneak me some food anyway, especially rainbow sherbet
in its neat little pleated paper cup. The sherbet is summer
and the sherbet is the Granit, and the more I think
about the sherbet and how soupy it will be by the time it gets to me,
well, I throw the crinoline over my head
and pray to God no one will notice it's underwear.

Eppes Essen

We walked into Greenspans in Jersey City
on Sunday nights when my mother looked forward
to *lungen* stew and I chewed on *kishka's* elastic skin
even after I learned it was cow intestines.

On special Friday nights or on *yontif* my mother
made a porridge of beef, barley, and vegetables
using cow knee bones for stock and she'd set aside
the bones for me, the fat hanging off the sides,
oozing from the hard-to-get middle, teasing
and tantalizing my taste buds. The bones
kept me busy for hours. To save them
for me when my mother preferred them
for herself demonstrated her love.

The butcher in Irvington entered the house on Thursday
to deliver chicken feet and *eyerlach*—unhatched eggs
taken from slaughtered chickens—which did not
then disgust me, although I still recoil at runny egg yolks.
Nothing compares with the inviting scent of rendering
chicken fat, the *gribenes* frying in the blue-marbled cast iron pan
and my mother's preparations with her wooden bowl
and chopper. Knowing that for Shabbos we'd have
an appetizer of eggs and onions, bound together
with my mother's tireless *shmalz*.

Today when I enter one of the few kosher restaurants left
I know it's not en vogue to want, let alone order, the fatty
substances that bring back my childhood. Paper strips
now wrap *kishka*. How can the name translate
to "stuffed derma" when there's no skin? Greenspans
is long gone. Butchers don't sell knee bones or *eyerlach*.
Health concerns have overwhelmed taste and tradition.

Only remnants exist. Chicken soup with no meat, please.
Matzoh balls (light and fluffy), *kreplach* (if you can find them
fresh), chopped liver (made from my mother's recipe, not
too smooth), and the Sloppy Joe. Not the Manwich
imitator, but the triple-decker with turkey, roast beef,
and either pastrami or corned beef with coleslaw
and Russian dressing. Not that the Sloppy Joe tastes
the same as when my father delivered our New Year's Eve
platters direct from Greenspans. Today only lean cuts
are possible. No taste. Fat is necessary, people. When I
see fat or poultry skin lingering on a dining companion's
plate, it takes all my willpower not to snatch it.
My arteries are probably already hardened, although
that would be the least of my health problems. If I'd
ever be able to eat the real stuff again, I'd have to arm
myself with Nexium and Tums. It would be worth it.

Bei Mir Bistu Shayn

The Andrews Sisters sing on the radio
while she poses for the photograph. She
lifts three fingers to her chin, wrist bent,
the platinum onyx-diamond ring her papa
gave her dead center. But he would never say,

"*Bei mir bistu shayn.*" Not one compliment.
"You should go out and change the world,"
he'd say. She's happy enough with the ring.
Her hair's done up Betty Grable-style
with a bit of lace like baby's breath pinned
to her crown. The black and white photograph
will not capture her blood red nails, blood red lips.

She'll send Milton the picture. He'll slip
it into his wallet at first to keep it safe. She
could teach him manners. Even in that foreign
land of Jersey she knows he'll be a good provider.

"*Bei mir bistu shayn,*" he'll say to her
and mean it, his eyes misting. He encases the photo
in a silver frame against magenta foil with
a four-bullet flank. He places it
on top of the bedroom TV console.

Years later, as she lay dying at Clara Maas, I
stroke her forearms, soothe her paper-thin
temples. I call her *Shayne Leah*. She grasps all of me.

She watches over me from her place fronting
my dresser mirror. Mama, *bei mir bistu shayn*.
You'll always be beautiful.

Quilted

I curl into a fetal position under my paisley quilt
while my sisters watch *Wheel of Fortune*
and our mother lies breathless, readying for burial.

Alone in an upstairs bedroom in an 1850 farmhouse,
Calkins Creek burbles beneath my window. I try
to write but I suffer from what my mother would call
nichtgutkeit and there is no cure except assuming
a fetal position under the rose-patterned quilt.

Along the labyrinth paths in Lenox, Mass., I pick up
stones and wonder which one I should place
on my mother's grave. I bring several home and place
them in a bowl under a plastic sign from my mother's
house that says *Shalom* in Hebrew.

Standing, sitting, lying I practice rolling up my
vertebrae to one day get back under my mother's quilt.

My Mother Was Dead

my mother was dead
and I took a plane to Poland
and walked on the streets
where her mother padded barefoot
or rode in a wagon before
asphalt covered the gravel.

my mother was dead
and I asked her dead mother,
help me find our family graves
in the cemetery with no headstones,
and I found crumbles of stone
with faded Hebrew lettering
the Nazis forgot to take.

my mother was dead
and I awoke on a crisp September morning
on the anniversary of the day
the Ostrova Jews were murdered
with my windows thrown open
to the sounds of school children and roosters
and a town waking up.

my mother was dead
and I walked the paths of Zaromb
and entered the yellow house with the loft
I told myself belonged to her father
where his father practiced religious calligraphy
and his mother grew cucumbers
in the field they rented from the glazier.

my mother was dead
and I couldn't tell her what I had seen
and even with the pine cones from the Zaromb forest
and the earth from the Ostrova cemetery
she would never know the home I found.

Elegy to Aunt Jo

Charlie's notice of your burial service caught me
off guard. But I remember that photo he included,
that one of you in a sleeveless brocade dress
in front of the mirror. The double image, perhaps
unintended, reminds me that you—like me—were a twin.

You told me once you could have gone to Brandeis,
but you didn't want to leave your home in Newark
or your twin. You married my uncle in '56, I don't know
what you expected. By then he was part-owner
of a grocery store with his brothers. You began to wear

your hair in a bee-hive, all starched with hairspray
and you told me Grandpa spoke beautiful Jewish
and I never really heard him speak at all. He coughed
phlegm while running around in his union suit. You
had a large white house in Caldwell and a lap dog

you named Shoo-Shoo and you bought me a hamster
I named Valentine and was actually relieved
when my uncle ran over it with his car in the driveway.
You invited me for sleepovers and for trips to the lake
to visit your sister and brother. You were brilliant

and beautiful but listless and showed up at my sister's
wedding in '73 in a pink jumpsuit and flirted with the judge.
You moved to California after the divorce and I visited
you in Marina del Rey. We held your Norwegian
granddaughter and posed for photos in the living room
with Amy's Christmas tree for backdrop. You stayed

in touch with my mother and I think she liked you.
You were interesting at least.

Twin Journey

In the darkness we take each other's hands and smile,
swim out and away, soaring above the woman who will be
our mother. We fly across the water, across the burnt
Mengele offerings we replace. We flitter above Poland
and our ancestors in unmarked graves. I want to touch
down and catch the white butterflies, but a rumble
startles me, us, and we know it's time to go back. My
sister lets go of my hand and heads toward the light
and I am left alone in the darkness, the pressure
of her fingers still intertwined with mine. I follow
and see her wrapped in pink. We reach toward each other
but are too far apart to touch. We wail.

First Memories

Helen, forcing us to walk to Robert Hall discount clothing
a mile away on the avenue.

Clara, locking us in our room for a nap with the lock
on the outside of the door. I help my twin sister out of her crib.
We destroy the room and poop in the toy chest.

Daddy, waiting for us at the bottom of the stairs
as we run to him, scarlet-fevered. He's not alone
and when we recognize Dr. Kagan, we scurry
back up the stairs until they catch us.

Grandpa Perlman, pulling us one by one onto his lap
for a horsey ride in his dark Bensonhurst apartment.
Grandma Perlman, pinching our *mamashaynele* cheeks
and cutting oranges into eighths.

Sheba, Freddie Hanson's German shepherd, peering
into our crib while our eldest sister flirts on the driveway.
The dog's face, inches away, we turn toward each other
for comfort, though Sheba gives me a lifelong fear of animals
and through hypnosis, I equate her with my ex-husband.
They slobber and drool the same way.

My sister remembers love and the feel of our mother's hand,
so much bigger and redder than ours. I remember
my father's Ivory smell and the feel of his hand. She remembers
herself alone. I remember us together.

Things in the Junk Drawer

Old Weight Watchers recipes, booklets,
and weigh-in cards that I'm too embarrassed
to open. Old eyeglasses and cases dating
back to when I bought this house in '92.
Unopened packages of black shoelaces
and a combination lock. A box of 48
Ticonderoga pencils and attachable erasers.
Pink and yellow customer receipts for big purchases—
window replacements when my son broke
one window after another, window blinds
when he ripped them down, Ethan Allan furniture
before he nicked it by banging a big-ass Russian
wooden spoon my ex-mother-in-law gave me. A
broken x-acto knife. My son's Marvin the Martian
telephone book with no entries—no addresses,
no phone numbers, no birthdays, because he had
no friends. A rolled-up, neon pink tape measure
to track my life. Train schedules between New Brunswick
and New York. Anything to keep me from home
and obligation and calls to the police.

When I Dream of Twisters

I'm not calling up Dorothy
or the Helen Hunt/Bill Paxton
movie. The skies threaten
with their green tinge, I call out
to you—my voice trying to scale
the wails of wind.

You had run out, oblivious to the storm.
You're not grown anymore. You're eight
and unmedicated. I can't find you.

You are the wind, the rain, the funnel that has already
sucked me into your vortex. There is no way out.

I want the dreams to end like that day at Epcot
when you ran off during the evening parade and I
wailed outside Security. You sauntered by
and said, "Hi, Mom."

Dirt

Take this shovel and plunge it deep into the earth's
chocolate cake, like the ones we used to make
outside on rainy days and pretend there was frosting,
the metallic taste lasting for days on our tongues.

Take this shovel and fill it now, hold it steady
with two hands. For this you'll have to put
your graveside prayer book in your pocket. Swing
the shovel to just over the grave and tilt the handle
slightly. The mound of dirt becomes a stream
of sparkles that plunks against the wood,
the earth and pine go so well together. Dirt gives
the wood comfort and cushioning like its own fleece blanket.

Others take their turns with the shovel until the entire
veneer of the casket is covered. Then the professionals
join in to cover it fully. You try not to think about
worms infiltrating the wood between the hinges and locks,
snaking their way through the silk lining and over
the decaying skin of the woman whose hand you once held,
who told you not to make those mud pies, because nothing's
worse than dirt-induced vomit. As long as it's done outside
it shouldn't matter. The dirt returns to the dirt and it's comfort.

Glossary

Alter Kocker—the old male
Bei mir bistu shayne—by me, you're beautiful
Bubbe—grandma
cholent—a stew made ahead of time for the Sabbath
DP—Displaced Persons
eyerlach—unfertilized chicken eggs
Frume—pious
gribenes—chicken or goose skin cracklings with fried onions
keinehora—a word to ward off the evil eye, usually followed with
three spits
kishka—a mixture of grains wrapped in cow's intestines
kreplach—meat-filled dumplings
lungen—lungs
mamashaynele—mother's pretty one, usually a child
mameloshn—mother tongue
nichtgutkeit—non-specific malaise
Rosh Hashonah—the Jewish New Year
Shabbos—Sabbath
shalom—Hebrew for hello or peace
shayne—beautiful
shmalz—fat (substance)
shiva—a seven-day period of mourning
shtetl—little town; usually refers to the Jewish villages of Eastern
    Europe
Sukkot—the Jewish holiday that celebrates the harvest
Tate—Father

Barbara Diane Krasner is an award-winning writer of poetry, fiction, and nonfiction for adults and children. She holds an MFA from the Vermont College of Fine Arts and an MA in History from William Paterson University, where she teaches creative writing, composition, and history. History inspires her poetry, which has appeared in numerous journals, including *Nimrod, Paterson Literary Review, Rust + Moth, Jewish Women's Literary Journal,* and *Blue Lyra Review*. She is the author of *Discovering Your Jewish Ancestors* (Heritage Quest, 2001) and served as contributing editor to *History Magazine* and two genealogy magazines. She publishes the popular blog, *The Whole Megillah | The Writer's Resource for Jewish Story* at http://thewholemegillah.wordpress.com. Her website is www.barbarakrasner.com.

www.ingramcontent.com/pod-product-compliance
Lightning Source LLC
LaVergne TN
LVHW051613080426
835510LV00020B/3277